THE
POP·UP
PARADIGM

HOW BRANDS BUILD HUMAN
CONNECTIONS IN A DIGITAL AGE

Melissa Gonzalez

THE POP-UP PARADIGM:
HOW BRANDS BUILD HUMAN
CONNECTIONS IN A DIGITAL AGE
ISBN 978-1-6196130-2-7

LIONCREST
PUBLISHING

www.lioncrest.com

I dedicate this book to my amazing
family, team, and strategic partners
who continue to believe in my vision.

Melugila
It was a
pleasure having you
on our team!
Sincerly
Melissa

contents

Introduction

In 2009, I made a decision to leave Wall Street so that I could pursue my passions. I was hosting a TV show and producing independent films, and had a relentless thirst for the creative world. Upon leaving, I stumbled upon an opportunity I never could have imagined...I was handed real estate space in midtown Manhattan at the Roger Smith hotel with the offer to "*do something creative.*" In the early part of my Wall Street retirement, I had begun a web series about beauty, fashion, and fitness where I often collaborated with emerging designers and interesting brands. What I quickly learned was that I brought something unique to the table with a combination of passion for the arts and design, along with an inherent savviness for business. Within one week of my pot-of-luck real estate offer, I began filling the calendar with extraordinary brands looking for the chance to have a storefront in NYC to build their businesses.

At the time of my new business's inception, e-commerce was just really beginning to take off, and many brands signing up for pop-ups barely had a functioning site. On the other side of the spectrum were a growing entourage of well-funded ideas and web-only stores beginning to make their mark in the physical world like Bauble Bar, GILT, Birchbox, Bonobos, and Rent the Runway. As companies like Shopify made creating an e-commerce store easier and easier, online stores proliferated, but the cost of customer acquisition created a very high barrier to success and profitability. Meanwhile, social media flourished (and continues to do so), and consumers became more connected, better informed, and savvier than ever before. While this occasionally overwhelmed them with options, it also equipped the consumers to find the best deals for themselves, whether it be price, quality, or ideally, both.

Given the evolution of commerce, being "online only" is no longer enough. It's highly expensive to show up in searches, dominate social media, deliver a well-branded message, and properly curate products that resonate with your audience. In a high-touch world, brands need a method to bridge the gap between online and offline interactions.

Whether you're just launching a brand, testing a new market, introducing something new, have a highly technical product that requires education, or want an isolated timeframe to show your customers appreciation, a well-planned pop-up store activation can allow you to deliver something unique to your audience. Sales will always be a goal — but unless you are doing a sample sale, it's probably a longer-tail benefit. More than just another way to sell product, a pop-up shop is a marketing tool. With the proliferation of mobile device usage, social media, and retail technology advancements, you will not only gain opportunities to interact with your core market, but will have a defined test period to collect data and learn more about your customers' needs, wants, and interests. It will give you information that impacts production, pricing strategy, merchandising presentation, homepage design, email marketing, and more. Putting your product in a customer's hand, within a lifestyle-branded environment with an opportunity to interact with the team behind the brand, is priceless.

In this book, we tackle some of the many ways that activating a pop-up shop can benefit your brand, from creating partnerships to learning about your customer. We also teach you how to do it effectively, creating a lasting impression by delivering experiences.

As Ron Johnson, former chief architect of Apple Retail Stores, perfectly said, "Go after mindshare, not market share."

This book will show you how.

PART

I

Where Retail's Been

one

The Evolution of Retail

Growing up, shopping was different from what it is today. There was no Amazon.com, and malls were shopping hub meccas bustling with activity, where retailers grew their brand and distribution channels by building out a larger brick-and-mortar presence. Major brands with deep pockets could afford to take the risk of building out new stores, and write-off high profile (high cost!) addresses as loss leaders in exchange for marketing benefits. Emerging brands struggled to keep up.

Customers learned about sales and discounts based on the advertisements they saw in mass market newspaper; certainly, there was no such thing as curated, personal email marketing. The term "SEO" was not even a whisper in a retailer's vernacular. The only version of pop-up stores we regularly saw were seasonal businesses, largely dedicated to holiday periods such as Halloween and Christmas. Brands did not have the ability to communicate in real-time and directly with customers, showing them such things as a behind-the-scenes design processes and mood boards.

With brick-and-mortar (and the shopping experience of my youth), the challenge became the increasingly high costs of long-term leases and the day-to-day of operating these stores. These fixed costs became a major hurdle in the quest for profits.

Further, the advent of the Internet brought an entirely new disruption and approach to retail, which put additional pressure on brick-and-mortar profitability. In comparison to a physical presence, a scaled e-commerce business was open 24 hours a day, lowered inventory carrying costs, and brought other advantages to both the retailer and the customer. This created a flywheel effect where we saw *foot traffic* continually decrease, while *web traffic* soared.

The numbers support this shift and are, in fact, quite staggering. According to a report from Green Street Advisors, a real estate and REIT analytics firm, about 15% of U.S. malls will fail or be converted into non-retail space within the next 10 years. On the flip side, the e-commerce business for U.S. retailers ballooned to $231 billion in 2013, and is expected to increase to $370 billion by 2017, according to statistics from Forrester Research.

BUT E-COMMERCE ISN'T ENOUGH

These days, with a Shopify account and a small initial investment in website design, almost anybody can launch an
e-commerce business. The lure of low start-up costs and the
thought of limited operating costs have driven many emerging brands into the online marketplace.

However, as e-commerce has grown it has also evolved. The
challenge is that the web has become a very crowded place. It's
incredibly hard to stand out and build a presence online, and
traditional tools for customer acquisition have seen increasing costs. If you want to have a really distinctive website and
strong lifestyle-branded image, you won't be just "putting
up a website" anymore. You'll need to invest in photography,
copywriters, editors and a team who understands how to
leverage SEO. And this doesn't even take into account the
costs of paid customer acquisition and marketing.

Competition within Google AdWords has quickly made this
option unaffordable for smaller brands. Hence, the next
option, which has gathered momentum in recent years, has
been social media channels such as Facebook and Pinterest.
However, like AdWords, the race to grow likes, followers, and
pins has quickly become more challenging as social media
has moved beyond the early adopter stage.

As this market has become more crowded, e-commerce has
begun to lose some of its benefits. Today, it takes a meaning-
ful budget, a lot of content creation, and a great deal of effort
to stand out in the world of e-commerce.

OMNI-CHANNEL RETAIL EMERGES

It's not surprising that the same principles that have long driven success in physical retail also apply to the online world: Know your customer. What is your differentiation? Your brand has to be nimble, able to adapt and listen to the customer, because customers are presented with so many options. You need to deeply understand what the core values of your customers are and how to resonate with them to make your brand stand out. Do you compete on price? Do you offer a better fit? What do you provide that customers can't find anywhere else? Retailers need to think about these sorts of questions carefully, because the answers are not always easy to identify.

Although e-commerce has, indeed, evolved, we still witness many shoppers who prefer the physical act of shopping with real goods in front of them that they can touch and feel. From fabric to sizing to human interaction, there are many reasons why a customer might prefer a brick-and-mortar shopping experience.

The challenge for brands going forward is keeping both sets of shoppers: those in your physical world and those in your e-commerce world. Brands must appeal to those who love to go into the store to see, touch, and smell what they're going to purchase, as well as those who love the ease of one-click buying. For this reason, many retailers are now realizing that in order to compete and excel in the long term, they need an omni-channel retail strategy.

A great example of this is Warby Parker. They initially took a web-only approach and grew their brand by offering lower prices and a great quality product in a way that disrupted the existing power in the market, Luxottica. However, as they looked for new customer acquisition avenues, they realized they needed to tap into physical retail space in order to bring the branded lifestyle experience that's impossible to fully translate online.

Warby Parker was enormously successful online. They used the "buy one, get one" incentive, along with extremely high quality products, to disrupt the eyeglass industry online. They had a clear, successful online strategy, but they soon realized that that wasn't enough. Today, they've turned to creating brick-and-mortar stores in addition to their online presence, because there's an element of that branded lifestyle experience that's impossible to fully translate online.

The bottom line is that a brand that only exists in the online world isn't enough anymore. Even if they don't have the ability or desire to launch their own brick-and-mortar stores like Warby Parker, brands are realizing that they need some physical presence. Whether through trunk shows, store-in-stores, or pop-up shops, brands are experimenting with new ways to create a physical space where they can interact with customers one-on-one.

Once of the most difficult pieces of an omni-channel retail approach is the need for consistency: *If I go to a store, I expect similar pricing to an online source, a vibe from employees that matches their online brand, and a similar selection of style.* A customer doesn't care if they're in your brick-and-mortar space or your online space — they expect to be treated consistently by your brand and to have a similar experience.

AN INTERACTIVE EXPERIENCE

It is easy to see how retailing has significantly evolved in just a few short decades. Things we once never imagined would be part of the marketplace are now so common that no one thinks twice about them. Click a few buttons on your phone to find and purchase new merchandise, have it shipped for free to your door the next day, or even go to the local store and pick up the item yourself, avoiding long lines on the check-out counter and getting it the same day. You can learn about products or services half a world away, asking experts and customer service agents questions in real time and getting answers instantaneously. All of this contributes to a marketplace in which we are flush with products, but starving for experiences.

It's not that the *quality* of the product isn't important — it always will be, and it's what establishes and sustains the relationship between a brand and its customer base that has evolved. However, given the proliferation of social media, customer reviews, and the amount of content constantly being put in front of today's shopper, there is a mountain of "noise" for products to overcome. In other words, something has to happen to make a product or service stand out.

One of the main ways this has been achieved is by focusing sharply on the interaction between the brand and the customer. Today's brands are paying more attention to this interactive element than ever before through channels like social media. Viewers can engage with brands on Facebook and reviewers on Yelp instantly tell a community of users their opinion on how a business is performing. People now want to be a part of the action, not just be told what to buy. A brand's job today is to establish a long-term relationship with their customers by delivering an experience that a person can truly be a part of.

You can see this increased interaction showing up in the physical world as well, with stores in forms that have never existed before like pop-up stores, pop-in stores, and mobile trucks. The purpose of these new retailer experiences is to make the shopping experience more personal and fresh. It's not just about hanging a product on a rack and waiting for the customer to find it. Today, brands are working harder to put that product into your closet.

There a number of ways that brands are trying to increase customer interaction in the real world, but more than anything else, temporary retail is thriving. According to a recent

Specialty Retail report, it is now an $8 billion industry that has grown 16% annually since 2009.

It is this last point that will be the focus of this book. Pop-up retail is a growing trend because it can be extremely effective, but it's also frequently done in the wrong ways for the wrong reasons, leaving brands disappointed with the result. Let's discuss this growing trend and how it solves the problems discussed in this chapter before exploring the ways in which your brand can leverage pop-up shops to get closer to your customer.

two

Bridging the Gap: The Pop-Up Paradigm

There are plenty of reasons why a brand could do a pop-up, and plenty of benefits to reap from it, both for the brand and the customer.

Let's say a brand is really big in Texas, but they want to make sure that New York will respond well to them before they actually move there. They'll want to test the new market and the neighborhoods within that market. Maybe they try something in SoHo, and then in Midtown, before they decide on a long-term lease. Using a pop-up shop to test these neighborhoods protects the brand from the major upfront spend of a long-term lease until they know if a city will work for them.

Pop-up stores can also be a great focus group for a product offering. It's a confined scope, so it really allows a brand or retailer to dive deeply into key performance indicators (KPIs). Maybe they have 30 products, but they really want to highlight a quarter of them in a curated collection. So they'll do a pop-up to gain awareness and a following for something that's new, something that's fresh, something that's different, or something that's very specific to a certain relationship. They'll end up with plenty of qualitative information to help them make decisions.

They will learn what the customer gravitates to, what colors get the most pre-orders and interest, what styles aren't resonating, and the price points that move quickly.

Sometimes, a retailer may want to grow their brand awareness and their social media presence and will use social media coupled with a pop-up as a strategic outlet to ignite user-generated content. From this, they are able to learn about the kinds of images their customers are posting about them. Whom are they influencing? In what social media channels are they posting the most? How many responses are they getting? These observations can inform a company's long-term marketing strategies.

This was apparent with Old Navy's wildly popular $1 flip-flop vending machine pop-ups. The company rolled out 36 locations in New York and Los Angeles, with a campaign designed to encourage shopper chatter of the sale on social sites, such as Twitter and Facebook (a feeting frenzy, if you will). Women were asked to "tweet for feet" with the hashtag #**flipflophooray**. The campaign sold 9,000 flip-flops and generated thousands of posts across channels. They also learned about the language, whether positive or negative, that customers were using to discuss their brand.

In some cases, there might also be an educational element that's important to their brand. Maybe customers don't understand the technical aspects or the formulation of a product or what the benefits of that technology is. There's no better way to teach than to let customers touch the product.

When Nespresso went on their retail tour with pop-ups nationwide, guests were able to use the coffee algorithm, which asked them basic questions, such as: "Are you a morning person?", "Do you like earthy or nutty flavors?", and "Do you prefer coffee or espresso?" Customers lined up to take the test, and at the end, they discovered flavors that may not have otherwise selected, and a new pod was released. In turn, Nespresso learned more about their customer preference. All of this led to heightening the awareness of Nespresso machines for sale online and across major department stores once the pop-ups ended.

At other times, the cycle can be reversed, where a retailer activates its social media engagement to curate what is sold in a physical space. Nordstrom has been a consistent leader in the retail space, with innovative tactics that integrate the online and offline worlds. In 2013, they began labeling their "Top Pinned Items" in stores with a Pinterest logo, alerting shoppers of the most popular online items and utilizing that to drive in-store sales. Nordstrom's Pinterest has over four million followers, making the top pins a pretty reliable reflection of what American women are coveting at the moment. And women often trust the advice of other women.

There are tons of other reasons for brands to experiment with pop-ups, too. It could be because a brand has a new exciting collaboration — Adidas collaborating with Stella McCartney, for example — and they want to get people to associate the brand with a celebrity presence and create buzz before it hits stores. Or, there may be a major event happening — like the Super Bowl or the World Cup — and a brand wants to pop-up with a physical space that injects their brand in the middle of a highly trending conversation in an authentic setting for hardcore fans that shop their line.

HOW CUSTOMERS BENEFIT FROM THE POP-UP PARADIGM

Customers crave human interaction. It's one of the main reasons that pop-ups are so powerful: they provide a ton of opportunity for face-to-face contact.

If it's a brand that's been created by an emerging designer, for example, customers often get the opportunity to meet the person creating it and learn the design story and their passions behind it. They really feel like they're supporting a new friend.

On the other hand, for brands like Warby Parker or Birchbox with a "cult" following that's been built entirely online, pop-ups can allow customers to experience the brand in person for the first time.

Another benefit for customers comes from brands like J.Hilburn, who use pop-ups where men can meet their stylist, get measured, and enjoy the fully customized experience. These pop-ups allow men who are concerned about fit to feel comfortable buying shirts online.

Perhaps your offering needs higher touch education, such as the Ministry of Supply's shirts and socks for men, which have phase change technology that acts like a battery, storing heat away from the body when overheated, and releasing it back when you return to an air-conditioned office so you stay at your ideal body temperature. Creating a pop-up where customers can test your advanced technology for themselves, see how amazing it is, and meet the brains behind the invention can be truly powerful.

Incentives and rewards can be tied into these experiences, so customers get an extra bonus for interacting with the brand. The Daisy Marc Jacobs Tweet Shop is an amazing example. It was Fashion Week, and visitors to the Tweet Shop got to interact with the brand in ways that weren't possible unless they could get into Lincoln Center. Customers participated and had a voice in the coveted Marc Jacobs brand, and they received a gift for doing it! It was a win-win situation, and customers couldn't believe it.

And, of course, there's also the possibility of meeting celebrities, like at the Nordstrom — Sarah Jessica Parker Pop-Up store, where customers had the opportunity to meet the woman from *Sex and the City* who had the best shoe collection ever. Not only that, but she was working the store and helping people try on their shoes and find the right fit. Can you imagine what a hit that was?

These are all huge selling points for the customer, who is not just a number shopping a product, but a person really getting entrenched in the experience of the brand.

Brands can do a lot of fun, interesting, inventive things in a pop-up – where it's more short-term – that they can't do in a full-time retail location. It allows them to really focus on that isolated "moment," whether that moment lasts for four days or a month. Most of these experiences exist to serve the customer.

Customers today have a different level of expectations from a pop-up store than a regular store. They expect to be delighted. They expect to either get a deal, or at the very least, something unique and different. Brands and retailers are expected to produce something creative in a physical space.

The customer gets an experience that feels uniquely different. It's not just about having a pop-up store because you have an end-of-the-season sample sale or a seasonal business. *Brands are learning to use pop-ups to interact with their customers in new and engaging ways.*

SAVVY CUSTOMER APPEAL

Customers are so much savvier now than ever before. They're all on social media. They're price shopping. Even demographics that aren't so internet savvy have seen and been exposed to so much information now that there's no fooling them. They're looking for that brand connection and experience.

Customers also use technology more now for comparison shopping, getting educated, reading reviews, seeing what their friends think, and knowing what else is out there before they make their buying decisions. Even with the inherent impulse to buy because of the short pop-up timeframe, customers have a deeper, wider breadth of knowledge within any given category in order to make those decisions.

It could be shoes. It could be cupcakes. It could be technology or electronics. They're asking, "What are my other options? Where else are they being sold? How much do they cost? What do the reviews say? What are my friends saying about it? " All that information is at a customer's fingertips now.

Brands need to go back to the point that customers are at pop-ups *for experiences, not products.* They walk through the door more with a mindset of, "What's fresh, new, and different that I'm going to learn today or get to experience by coming into this pop-up?", versus walking into the store that's open year-round, where they're asking, "Okay, what new products do you have?"

USING DELIGHTED CUSTOMERS TO FIND MORE CUSTOMERS

A pop-up will also be a great way to attract new customers by activating your existing customer base to do your marketing.

Johnnie-O does a great job of this each year when they open their summer pop-up shop on the East Coast to bring West Coast Prep to NYC. We work with them to pre-craft a calendar of events where they collaborate with on-brand partners and host spotlight nights for existing customers throughout the month of June. They partner with brands such a Sprinkles Cupcakes and Question Tequila to serve surfer dude cupcakes and slushy margaritas in their beach-themed store setting, complete with a sandy beach window, a cooler filled with ice cold beer, golf clubs and other aspects of the surfer dude lifestyle. This all adds an element of authenticity to the experience for the guests.

Customers are incentivized to take photographs and share them on their social media channels;. Bloggers love it and all the brands benefit from co-promotion. They also have a huge collegiate following, and each year when they co-host college nights with their college brand ambassadors, it's a packed house because every invited guest brings two or three friends.

The uniqueness of the experience makes their existing fan base excited to promote the brand.

PART

II

What a Pop-Up Offers Your Brand

three

Pop-Up Goals

Part of the beauty of a pop-up shop is that it exists in an isolated timeframe where you have a limited downside. The pop-up shop allows you to achieve multiple goals in a temporary setting, using a relatively low-cost alternative to investing large sums of capital in order to sign multi-year leases and make other long-term commitments.

The first thing to remember is that not all pop-up events are intended to sell merchandise. Likewise, not all pop-up events are intended to launch a brand. Pop-up activations are ultimately about customer engagement. They are an opportunity to physically interact with customers, surround them with your message and gather feedback about your customer at the same time.

What makes pop-up events special is that they are unique

to your brand and goals, so there is no one formula that will work for everyone. However, some questions to ask when identifying the goals of your pop-up should include:

- Are you launching a new brand or category within an existing brand?
- Are you growing brand awareness for a specific product line?
- Are you testing a new market?
- Are you experimenting with what works and what doesn't?
- Are you educating customers?
- How will you immerse them in the lifestyle experience of your brand?
- Are you testing the launch of a new partnership or collaboration?
- Are you flushing out inventory with a sample sale?
- Are you leveraging a highly seasonal business?

The answers to these questions will inform you as to what your plans and strategy should be for your pop-up shop. They'll allow you to hone in on what your purpose is and what your customers' expectations might be. By having clearly defined goals and expectations, you'll be able to focus on building out a true experience for your customers.

In a way, a pop-up is an amplification of a focus group. It allows you to collect a substantial amount of information on customer reactions to a product and it creates an environment in which people are giving you feedback. However, they are also speaking publicly about it, and even sharing it on their social channels. They're not sitting in a small group where they feel confined to give you structured answers. They're coming to discover a new experience and talk about how it makes them feel.

Step one when planning your brand's pop-up shop is to step back and think about your key goals. There's lots of possible benefits, but what's the one goal that this pop-up needs to achieve to be a success?

So, even though it's more public, it's also a safe environment created for them. They're excited that they can give feedback to a company and really have a say. Potentially, this company will even make adjustments, upgrades, or improvements based on what the customer has said. People are more likely to give honest feedback when they feel like they actually have a voice.

If you are launching a new brand, it's a great way to learn what resonates with your projected target market. If your brand already has a presence in one city but you want to explore another, it's a test to be sure you open in the right neighborhood and an opportunity to learn how merchandising and pricing may be impacted from city to city.

Brands can explore completely different audiences with

pop-ups, too. For example, just because you might be a great men's retailer doesn't mean that you can't sell equally well to women. You can potentially use the pop-up as a cross-marketing opportunity, combining with existing interest groups of *women who are shopping for your target male demographic*. In a pop-up, a brand has a safe place to test new markets, customers, and beyond.

Williams-Sonoma, Inc. is an example of a company that uses pop-ups well with their teen market tests. They utilize pop-ups to see what's resonating with the teens before they really move forward on full production of a new line. It's successful for them because they have an isolated timeframe to learn about a product's potential before investing heavily in it. It also helps inform the online marketplace: If Pottery Barn Teen has a pop-up store that can track and collect data about what the teen market is purchasing in-store, they can make educated guesses on what lines/products to put into full production for e-commerce.

In this way, pop-ups allow brands to learn in a cost effective way what people are willing to pay for, and can use this information to decide what they're actually going to put dollars behind in the coming season. These pop-ups can get pretty specific, too. We once worked with a brand from New Orleans that wanted to test new markets before deciding on their second permanent location. They decided to test New York, but with a spin: They made almost everything out of cork! They made cork handbags, cork umbrellas, cork golf bags. It was truly impressive. From their six-week pop-up, they learned the challenges of the New York market and how the customer there differed from New Orleans.

Furthermore, pop-ups today are not just in retail stores. They're everywhere, in almost every industry. We've seen pop-up hotels, pop-up restaurants, and pop-up malls. Pier 57 in New York City, for example, is under development for a pop-up village of shipping containers called Super Pier, off the West Side Highway. Even hotels are realizing that they don't need to be open year-round. They can create an isolated host experience and test the market before they decide if they want to have the long-term hotel in a specific location.

The possibilities are continuing to evolve with how brands are popping up. The possibilities are endless. In this section of the book, we will cover the various benefits that pop-ups can provide for brands and retailers in more detail. No matter what your business is, this section should spark some ideas in your mind for ways in which activating a pop-up might benefit it.

Launching a
New Brand

As we've discussed, pop-up shops are about creating an experience that allows you to connect with customers in a physical space and communicate your brand message. When you are a newly launched brand, the clarity of that message is crucial. Your first pop-up is also the first face-to-face impression you will create with the press and customers, and it must be clearly defined and presented.

First, you will want to take time to ensure that the actual physical space tells a story that will make a lasting impression on customers and the media. The first impression of your pop-up shop can determine whether or not people will explore your brand and product offering further. Starting with a storefront that connects with naturally occurring foot traffic and drawing them in and continuing through a well-designed interior space with "speed bumps" to keep their attention, the environment needs to meet or exceed their expectations by immersing them in an authentic experience.

Whether you have 50 square feet or 5,000, you need to invest time and money in your design. It doesn't have to be a realistic experience, or a practical experience, but it needs to evoke an emotional connection to your brand. Creating an impactful pop-up experience starts with an honest assessment of your company and your brand. Start by asking yourself the following questions:

- What does your brand (or company) stand for? What is the brand message?
- Describe your customer. Who are they? Who do they want to be? What are the barriers between these two states that your brand or company helps remove?
- Are there required elements that need to be worked in for your brand? Does your brand have established logos or service marks that need to be represented?
- What is the environment that best suits your brand message? Ultramodern? Traditional? Rustic?
- What action would you like every visitor to take? Share on social networks? Make a purchase? Join a mailing list? This ties into the purpose that we established when planning the pop-up.

The answers to these questions can help you identify exactly how you want people to feel when they enter your space, and exactly what you want them to do once they are there.

Creating an impactful pop-up experience starts with an honest assessment of your company and your brand.

You will want to find merchandising and display pieces that complete a holistic design message. For example, do regular silver racks make sense or do shadow boxes and silver pipes display your collection better? Every piece of shelving and furniture is there to further your brand, so choosing pieces that serve as the perfect displays for your merchandise is essential. The key is to make your presentation fluid and clean to showcase your offering without feeling cluttered, so be sure to leave duplicates and extra pieces in your back storage area and replenish as needed.

As an example, jewelry designer K-Kane did a great job of this when she launched her first pop-up shop with us. She had a dedicated wall designed with clear messaging, educating the customer on how her monogram process works. She filled the shelves with lifestyle elements of the women who would wear her brand, including beautifully carved jewelry boxes, flower arrangements, and books. It conveyed luxury, but in an approachable way and established a level of trust as soon as you walked in the door.

Get creative with your merchandising displays, as it will add to what makes the experience feel unique. A couple of online sites for inspiration are Pinterest (you can search "retail displays") and WindowsWear.com (a great destinations to search for some of the best window displays from across the globe).

Keep in mind the idea that you need to "immerse" people in your brand, while also keeping the focus on the purpose of your store. Once you've grabbed people's attention (outside) and immersed them in your brand (inside), return your focus to the purpose of your product, and have a plan to convert your pop-up guests based on the actions your purpose requires.

five

Customer Engagement

While the notion of a pop-up store may still be a little new to you as a brand or a retailer, the notion of customer engagement isn't — it's what a brand is all about. Assuming that people already know your story is a mistake, and in these socially-interactive times, assuming people will express themselves about your brand, without a reason, can be an even bigger one.

Customer engagement allows for a couple of key interactions. First, it allows customers to experience your brand on a whole other level. Second, and sometimes more importantly, it empowers them to feel like they're involved in the brand. They begin to feel that their voice is a part of the brand. You see it all the time: customers at a store taking pictures of themselves, which they're posting on social media with a hashtag. This really allows customers to "inject" themselves into your brand, and pop-ups can provide them with a truly unique opportunity to do so.

Aruba Tourism's "Pop-up Paradise" was an example of just that. In the middle of Times Square on Valentine's Day, Aruba Tourism set up a booth for people to renew their vows. It was perfect: a romantic beach area where people could renew their vows and take a picture of what they would look like in Aruba doing that very thing. By appealing to people's fantasies, the pop-up paradise resulted in hundreds of social media postings. The best part? Some of the participants got free trips, so they *could* do it for real!

That was a huge way for people to immerse themselves in this conversation about love, Aruba, and traveling. It got into people's psyches and formed a connection between the words "love" and "marriage" and "romance" and "Aruba" — even the thousands of people who weren't there but were reached through social media.

Brands need to encourage these kinds of customer engagements for many reasons, but one major reason is that the customer's point of view becomes, "*I have a voice, too.*" In this way, you create real evangelists for your brand, because they feel like they are part of the experience of the product: "*Look at the picture I posted. Look what I got for it. They valued what I had to say.*"

Pop-ups built upon customer engagement empower customers to inject themselves into your brand, and provide them with a truly unique opportunity to do so. By making customers proud and excited to act as brand ambassadors, you can trust them to do your marketing for you.

CAN'T THESE EXPERIENCES BE CREATED ONLINE?

Many brands ask, "But can't we do the same thing online?"

There is an aspect of this type of experience that fares well online: the brand can put up aspirational imagery and give awards and host contests — so, yes, the answer is that you can do a lot of this online. However, in an actual physical space, you can accomplish all that and more. When a customer participates in a pop-up, they are literally walking into the life of the brand. While they might have reluctantly tweeted about your brand for one day, receiving an invitation to share your real experience with the brand is much stronger. You satisfy the touch/feel gap, which creates a much stronger engagement with you as a brand.

THE TOUCH/FEEL GAP

An actual physical experience gives customers something they can't get online: an experience in all five senses. Online, you can certainly see a product, and even though people are trying to develop technology to enable you to touch and feel a product, it hasn't happened yet! When it comes to the aesthetics of a brand, there's no substitute for the genuine article, the real physical experience of being surrounded by the brand's promise.

We don't pay attention to just touch or feel, either. Notice how often when you're in a certain store, it even *smells* a certain way? Certain restaurants and clubs are famous for using trademark scents that customers associate with them. Luxury body and bath shop, Sabon, is the classic example of this. The way they involve a customer with the touch, feel, and smell of the product immediately leaves the customer with all five senses influencing how they feel around the brand. It's a total package.

Also, don't forget the opportunity to hear from, and speak to, a designer or brand ambassador. Yes, you can chat with some-body online, but it's not the same as an in person meeting.

So the "touch/feel" gap is actually much bigger than even one sense — it encompasses all of them. What you see, what you hear, and what scent surrounds you all contribute to how you feel about a brand. These things can't be replicated online.

DESIGNERS, STARS, AND OTHER BRAND CELEBRITIES

Having a celebrity involved in any pop-up is a great way to get customers excited and spur engagement. We mentioned the experience of the Sara Jessica Parker shoe store earlier, which is a great example. The good news is that your brand doesn't have to have a big-name celebrity or star on-hand to provide a great interactive experience in real time.

Customers are always going to have questions about your brand. That goes without saying. And while some of their questions can be answered online, an answer from a real person means a lot more.

That's why the best brands will often have a designer or a creator on-site to interact with customers. It's not just a salesperson answering your questions — it's the person who understands the design process and the meaning behind each piece. It's the passion behind why this particular product was created — its story. Then, when a customer asks, "Does this fit me?" he or she's got an answer that goes far beyond yes or no.

One example of this is NFP Studio, where a pop-up store introduced customers to the designer, Gail Travis. People say to their friends, "Oh, my friend Gail's back," and they bring people with them to meet this woman every time she does a pop-up...and sales skyrocket! Her customers understand her passion and her design process. They feel a kinship with her and want to support that.

Let's face it, we all love being allowed to "go behind the curtain." That's the feeling that meeting a designer or the person behind a brand provides. It makes customers want to buy into the story and the process, as they feel important and lucky for getting the opportunity. They feel like they've walked into a VIP experience, and that's tough to do in normal retail.

This all contributes to customers becoming what brands really treasure: an ambassador. It all comes from having a delightful experience that they can't wait to share.

USER-GENERATED CONNECTIONS: THE DAISY MARC JACOBS TWEET SHOP

As discussed earlier, a great example of this was the Daisy Marc Jacobs Tweet Shop. The idea behind the shop was that fans and customers would be able to pay with tweets or Instagram photos. It didn't matter how many followers you had, or your Klout Score rankings. All you had to do was participate.

"Anyone with a smartphone can do it...That's what I love about it," said one guest shopper quoted in *The New Yorker*. By snapping photos and posting messages with the hashtag #MJDaisyChain, visitors were awarded with Marc Jacobs-branded gifts. The feedback was incredible, and visitors were astonished that the brand was really valuing their involvement.

Remember the example of the Aruba pop-up in Times Square? Who doesn't want to feel excited and reminded of love and romance during Valentine's Day, and to be able to share that and pretend that they're on a beach in the middle of Times Square? That idea was such a huge success because of the great positive message, and users willingly shared the message because of it.

Another brand that did a great job encouraging customers to become ambassadors was Belvita, with its "morning win" program. They invited people to come online and post their morning triumphs each day. It could be anything: getting up early, going for a run, eating a healthy breakfast, or whatever else constituted a successful morning. Afterward, people were contacted by the brand, saying, "We loved your triumph this morning. We're making you a Belvita trophy. Come pick it up from the store." People loved being patted on the back for achieving what they did that day. In the process, Belvita became associated with triumph and with winning. It was genius in that it took a situation that people were already tweeting or posting and turned it into something exciting and fun that involved the brand.

In order to invite effective customer engagement, the most important factor is that a brand deeply understands the customer. Pop-ups need to appeal to something that customers really want to participate in so that they are motivated to join the conversation.

THE ASPIRATIONAL CONNECTION

What makes people want to share images online? What makes them proud of the picture they're putting up? What makes them excited enough that they'll decide to become ambassadors for your brand?

Customers get excited about situations that, in most cases,

aren't attainable. You don't normally get to shop with Sarah Jessica Parker, and so that's a dream come true for lots of people. How often does somebody that you watch on TV help you to try on your shoe? That's a pretty big hook, and it inspires you to want to tell everybody you know. Something that you can't normally get every day, something *aspirational*, is what turns the key. *I aspire to win the morning. I aspire to be in paradise. I aspire to...whatever.* Fill in the blank!

Aspirational is a great umbrella word: it covers a lot of territory. In order to be aspirational, a brand needs to really know their customer. This allows them to evoke key emotions — love, or romance, or being empowered to be more fashionable, to be on the cutting edge — and allow their customer to identify with that emotion and to share this feeling with their friends. So, in that way, a pop-up store can turn create an aspirational connection and, in turn, *inspire conversations about your brand.*

six

Focused Learning and Testing

THE POP-UP "TEST KITCHEN"

Another major way brands use pop-up shops is in the area of focused testing — testing concepts, locations, or new ideas. We all know about test kitchens: food purveyors use them all the time. There's even a TV show called *Restaurant Kickstart* on CNBC where candidates compete for Kickstarter funds to open a pop-up restaurant.

Brands use pop-ups to test lots of "ingredients" in their product mix. They could be testing usability of a product. They could be analyzing customer engagement, price point sensitivity, or color choices, or even which street they should be on or which climate they should be in.

How do these tests work? First, the brand clearly defines the question. Then, by keeping a certain number of constants, they begin changing variables and collecting data to learn what works and what doesn't.

USING ALL THE TOOLS, PART 1: TECHNOLOGY AND DEMOGRAPHICS

Say, for example, a brand wants to test colors — which color sells more to what kind of customer. The good news is that technology already allows for ways to collect data: a POS system, sensors, or a photo booth. Then, they stock the store and look at the reports at the end of the day, or at the end of a given period of time, and draw conclusions: *Okay, this color and that color we put on the shelves all sold. This other color didn't.* Maybe they realize that red is the top color in city A, so they should have deeper inventory there versus black, which is maybe a better seller in city B. That can be fashion-based or trend-based.

What else do they track? They can analyze sales based on the way a window was designed from one week to the next. Maybe during week one the window display had a lot of bright colors, and in the next week, it was black and white. How did that translate into not only bringing foot traffic inside but also actually converting those people into sales?

These are great data points from people that brands and retailers can collect.

The time of day can also make a difference. If people are online in sufficient numbers after the store closes, the brand can choose to send out their newsletter at a time that will target those customers. If a certain time of day brings in more foot traffic, you can bet the brand is going to plan accordingly. The weather and climate play a role, too. This will all have a significant impact on how they merchandise each product and where.

All of these things are possible, and often done, in standard retail locations. However, pop-ups allow brands a short time frame and a blank slate to experiment like crazy and really focus on learning about their customer. They also allow for online only brands, who have their own analytics but miss a lot of the data that can be gleaned in person, to venture into this form of testing.

USING ALL THE TOOLS, PART 2: LANGUAGE, CONVERSATION, AND SOCIAL MEDIA

Social media campaigns become more important every day. Smaller brands that have more conservative budgets can use systems such as TagBoard.com or OneQube to track the success of their social campaigns. These tools are free or very inexpensive to use. Sites like these allow a brand to watch the evolution of the conversation surrounding their brand from before the doors open until after the doors close, and manually check who was influential and sharing, and what they were saying.

Brands with larger budgets can work on bringing in state-of-the-art photo booth companies, such as Fotofwd, or innovative technologies, like Stylinity's selfie mirror cataloging system. With these technologies, brands end the day with a complete picture: "*Okay, this is our hashtag. These are all the people that shared. This is **where** they shared the most. This is **what** they shared. This is where it got the most interaction. These were our **top influencers**.*"

In addition, brands can also collect data on what words were said most often — positive or negative — in association with a designated hashtag during that activation. It could give them a lot of feedback along the lines of what their customer cares about. "*Maybe something different really inspired them other than what we thought it would be. This is the reason that made them hesitate to convert.*" Or perhaps you learn: "*There's a whole segment of fans out there that we didn't even realize existed.*"

One great example of this is an emerging designer brand, Nora Garnder Apparel. We have done two pop-ups with her thus far and are signed on to do a third in the coming spring season. She first came to us with a mindset that her customer was right out of college, millennial, super connected on social channels and looking for her first dress for the office. She stocked the store with fashionable colors, with a modern cut and shorter hemlines. She did okay, but quickly learned that it wasn't the woman in her twenties that was engaging and shopping, it was an older demographic, women 35+ on average that already had a career and knew what they wanted: something more classic and more forgiving in fit than the products she was selling.

Nora quickly digested the feedback and less than a year later came back for her second pop-up store, targeting the new demographic with modified styles, cuts, colors and fabrics. As a result, she more than tripled her sales. In fact, her new products sold so well that she covered all of her costs within the first week of her one month pop-up. She learned she needed to appeal to the woman that is a world traveler, is busy, and wants a cut that is reliable. And she is adjusting her social media strategies accordingly, focusing more on Facebook and newsletters rather than Instagram and Twitter.

A TALE OF TWO CITIES: POP-UP PRICING TESTS

A brand we mentioned earlier from New Orleans was testing the New York market and learned a few interesting things — among them, that the style, the average cart size, and the price point sensitivity was utterly different from the market where they had been.

Now, granted, you're going from New Orleans to New York City, so you may think, "Oh, obviously they're different clients." You might be surprised to find out, however, that a lot of the time, brands — at least some of the smaller ones — don't think that way. Their brand is their brand, and they don't realize that they need to change things until it's too late. The pop-up, then, allows some of the smaller brands to learn a little bit about the new market before diving in.

In the case of our New Orleans brand, they learned that they attracted more of the French Quarter "touristy" kind of shopper, motivated to shop more on impulse. They then went to New York and got a blend of the touristy shopper, *plus* the professional woman who actually lived in New York City. These people couldn't believe how inexpensive the product line was — and it was the same product line deemed borderline expensive in New Orleans.

They learned information beyond price as well: colors such as red brick and deep hues sold really well in New York, while in New Orleans, different types of colors did better. The cross-body bags and clutches used for going out and walking the street resonated really well in New York; down south, it was a different style that was selling, because women were using it differently. They drive cars. It's just a different lifestyle.

The average cart size was healthier in New York, too, than it was in New Orleans. During the month of the pop-up, in fact, the brand's top city of driving traffic to the site was New York, with New Orleans becoming number two. So the brand learned valuable information about pricing structure, merchandising, marketing, and what types of marketing tactics appeal to New York versus New Orleans.

POP-UP STAFF VERSUS PERSONAL STYLISTS: J.HILBURN'S TEST

J.Hilburn, a Dallas-based online retailer, did a test in New York. Traditionally, if you go to their site, you'll be assigned to a personal stylist who will contact you directly, meet with you in person, get your measurements, show you swatches of patterns and colors, and then you can order.

When the first outfit arrives and you see how well it fits, and you can easily reorder with the brand because you know your sizing and that there's a custom fit. For men, fit matters a lot: if they find something that fits, they keep buying it — unlike women, who tend to want to know what the next hot trend is. By stressing that quality fit, they were able to touch upon the core values of what that audience wants.

Next, they came to New York City with fully-merchandised outfits. Men could make an appointment with a stylist or they could just come in on their own. Once there, they could see how to mix and match ties with different shirt patterns, select the right jacket, and put together the whole ensemble for the complete look. The men were empowered by the stylist, learning how to mix and match colors and patterns and fabrics, where they might not have been so creative on their own online.

In this store that had well-merchandised outfits, and the customer was able to see everything. *"Oh, I own this shirt. That could go well with this, this, and that. Done. Order the whole outfit."* When J.Hilburn's customers didn't just learn their sizes, but actually how to put the full look together, their average store sale went up to $850, compared to $360 when it was just an online stylist.

POP-UPS THAT GO WHERE NO POP-UPS HAVE GONE BEFORE

Brands often use pop-ups to test more interior cities in the Midwest or South. Sometimes, it's highly successful; brands can be a big hit in locations where people don't normally have those options. For example, when GILT planned a pop-up shop in Louisville, it created a lot of excitement because people in Kentucky don't typically have access to something like that. The inventory sold very quickly.

Google did a pop-up in Minneapolis to tempt shoppers to learn more about interacting with the technology of the company. They called it a "Winter Wonderlab," with huge snow globes that visitors could step inside. They could make slow-motion videos and share them with their friends. From inside the Google Winter Wonderlab, you could create user-generated content, but you were also able to learn more about the Nexus 7, Chrome Pack, and Chromebooks that they were releasing in time for the holiday season. There was an educational element, true, but it was heavy on enjoyment. The message? *If you use this, you're going to have a lot of fun.*

In cities like New York, Los Angeles, and Chicago, the pop-up was a success. But in smaller locations like Paramus, New Jersey, it was a real hit. The people in Paramus aren't exposed to this kind of thing as often, so they appreciated it more. Because pop-ups are temporary, it's no longer necessary for brands to limit themselves to major cities.

SOME OTHER INNOVATIVE POP-UP TESTS

Mobile pop-ups: Veuve Clicquot, a leader in the luxury space when it comes to the pop-up concept, went mobile with Veuve Clicquot pop-up bars. #ClicquotMail is the hashtag for their pop-up truck, and over the course of the year, they partnered with key chefs, DJs and food venues across the world making the luxurious, upscale lifestyle accessible. Inspired by Madame Clicquot's correspondence style, snail mail, the glam trucks were decked out in the company's signature yellow color, traveling around the country and encouraging people to send handwritten letters to family and friends (an oh-so-enjoyable activity in this age of e-mail, texting, and FaceTime), while dispensing delectable appetizers like oysters and truffle fries, as well as Veuve samples.

Pop-up food trucks: This industry is no stranger to the power of mobile — pop-up restaurants have been popular since the 2000s in Britain and Australia — and now, with the emergence of social media, the industry has been empowered with the ability to use mobile street vendors to start and grow restaurants businesses. Mobile diners typically make use of social media, especially Twitter, to follow the movement of these restaurants. From breakfast, to lunch, to dinner, new businesses can travel from destination to destination serving new customers and growing their footprint.

Pop-in shops (store-within-a-store): Effectively used by Nordstrom, pop-in shops are a triple win for the retailer, brand, and shopper. With a store-within-a-store, brands are able to rent retail space inside an established retail store. "Pop-In at Nordstrom" is a series of themed pop-ups located inside the retailer's eight flagship locations. From this concept, they've learned what works well, when they can offer the high-to-low price point, and can pre-test introducing new designers and vendors to customers. Customers are able to come back and discover something new that genuinely taps their curiosity each visit.

WHEN GOOD POP-UPS GO BAD
Much of the time, the pop-up experience is positive. There are

times, however, when the brand might learn there's just not enough spending power in a particular area, or it's too "fashion-forward" for the region, or it wouldn't work year-round. It's good to know those things, too.

What happens if you crash and burn? Well, a "flop" can help a brand avoid a much more painful mistake, and it can even enhance your brand's presence in the long run. The key is in learning from what's happened.

Perhaps you had a shop in what seemed to be a great location — only it didn't cater to your target customer's actual presence in the area: where they live and work is different from where they spend their evenings. Knowing that, you can position future pop-ups better around the actual routine of your target customer.

Perhaps you had a great crowd and lots of buzz, but no sales spike. Open your eyes and ears to what feedback you hear during the experience, whether customers are talking about a price they don't like, a fit that isn't quite the thing, and so on. You can gain a lot of insight from surveying customers, either on the spot or afterward via e-mail or social media. Maybe a core element of your product doesn't resonate with the customer. This can teach you a lot and should impact your choice of materials, design, and price going forward.

Perhaps you thought the ambience and images were great, but your customers weren't sharing them, or they didn't drive traffic or sales. This is a case where you may be pushing what you think are all the right buttons, only to have a lukewarm reaction. While it may be easier to handle lukewarm rather than openly hostile reactions, the net result is the same — your brand isn't reaching and inspiring the people you want to reach and inspire.

Think back to the aspirational concept again, and pay attention to the words people use when they talk about your brand. If the images those words convey aren't what you're after, you'll need a better, clearer focus. Explore a collaboration with related products and think in terms of a bigger holistic experience. Use the words you hear about your brand to fine-tune the message you *want* to convey. Remember, it's always about the customer, and your pop-up activation gives you the opportunity to learn more about them and serve them better.

Sometimes failures can lead to successes. Properly analyzing why something failed allows a brand to rethink and better position going forward. The negative feedback is just as important as the positive.

seven

In-Depth Customer Education

Brands with complex offerings, new formulas, or a special mission can benefit from customers having an in-depth understanding of their product.

For example, Intel recently hosted a holiday shop detailing the features of their products, helping their customer really understand the differences of their technology and software offerings compared to its competitors. Lots of other brands have followed suit.

When you have a product that's so unique and different that you wouldn't get the whole story just from seeing it on the shelf, an educational pop-up can really hook a customer into the value proposition of your story. Most people aren't going to read the manual or documents explaining all the unique factors of the products that they're buying. They may watch videos and consume other versions of short-form media, but an educational pop-up goes a step farther: it lets them feel like they've walked into the laboratory.

An educational pop-up has a stronger impact than a manual, or even a video, because you're teaching them in a high touch environment. They're seeing the product, learning about what makes it unique, and they're getting to touch and feel it. You're involving a lot more senses to really dive deeply into what to differentiate, and they are getting to see real-time, hands-on, via live demonstrations. Plus, it's in a curated environment where a customer feels like this brand is educating them, not just selling them a product.

Canadian-based technology company, Shopify, has recently embarked on this strategy with a retail tour across major cities in Canada and the United States. Businesses who use Shopify for e-commerce, or who are thinking about it, have dedicated stores to visit where they can sign up for workshops and work side-by-side with experts and elevate how they utilize the technology via design, app integration, and more. Customers get to see all the cool features that Shopify has that can help their business, and they begin to see Shopify as more than just another online platform.

BEYOND THE RETAIL SET UP TO THE BRAND CLASSROOM

Brands simply can't teach everything in a normal retail situation. In a big store, Intel has a section, Google has a section, and Apple has a section, but you're not really solely focused on teaching why each device is different. You'd rarely see a targeted, centralized tutorial or workshop. In a pop-up that's focused on one product, the brand is able to create a community feel and a unique interest in that product.

Customers are coming in, speaking to someone in creative services, and getting to have a cup of coffee with them. They're giving you technology showcases. They're letting you touch and feel the product. They're letting you demo it with them. When you're in a larger department-store-type environment, it's really hard to dive that deeply into exactly what that product line is offering.

A pop-up shop is another way of having people listen to your story. You could pay for advertising and try to force people to listen or, instead, you can present this cool experience where people come into your world excited to hear your story.

The Timberland Earthkeeper pop-up experience is a great example of an educational pop-up. Not only did they have a new footwear line, but it was made out of recycled bottles and organic materials. You hear that all the time — about products being green — but seeing the transformation happen from start to finish is a whole other type of experience for a customer. Start with a bottle, end with a shoe! Inherently, they get the message that if they buy this product, they're a part of something cool, unique, and different.

It goes back to lifting the curtain. Now, customers get to step behind that design process and say, *"Oh, my goodness, I can give back by buying this product. It starts with a clear bottle, and it's coming out into a pair of shoes that I can wear, and I helped the environment, plus it looks good."* Now you've got a customer who is passionate about the product in more than one way — not just about the product, but about the entire experience.

FASHION PLUS FISH: THE KENZO POP-UP

Kenzo is a fashion brand that did a pop-up not unlike the Timberland example — only it wasn't as tied into the design of the product. Instead, it was about the brand being ultimately responsible and giving a message. It focused more on the aspirational notion we talked about earlier: it became a brand that people looked up to and admired because they cared about the environment.

They created an experience where they had an aquarium of fish where, little by little, the fish would disappear just as they would if you overfished in an environment. However, every time you bought a T-shirt, they'd put more fish back in the tank. Thus, they aligned themselves with an attitude that resonated with customers: *We want to be socially responsible, and by shopping with Kenzo, you're joining us in being socially responsible, too.*

GOING IN-DEPTH WITH BEAUTY

The beauty industry is very difficult, right? Fashion can

change on a whim. With beauty products, however, a customer usually has to invest in anything they decide to try for a certain period of time before they see any results. There's inherently a higher cost of change for a customer. Thus, this industry lends itself well to teaching the customer why the formulation of their product will be different from all the others, and why it's at least worth a try.

That's exactly what happened when SK-II hosted pop-up shops in New York City and San Francisco. The brand background: the story of SK-II began over 30 years ago in a chance discovery at a brewery, where scientists noticed that the sake brewers had wrinkled faces but youthful hands. The observation inspired research into the fermentation process, and after studying over 350 strains of yeast, a unique strain from which Pitera™ is naturally derived was discovered. In 2013, SK-II invited customers to experience their new Beauty Imaging System™ at their pop-up studios. Guests could visit for a complimentary personalized consultation that used their state-of-the-art skin analysis tool to provide an understanding of one's skin condition and help measure its progress over time. They walked out with new found knowledge and complimentary SK-II products. It established a relationship of trust based on education.

POP-UP PETS...

Pop-ups are terrific for other kinds of educational situations as well. Both the New York City Mayor's Alliance and the Animal Pet Foundation have done pet pop-ups. You come in, you learn about the pets, and you get to watch them on the webcam. You get hooked. You learn all about the adoption process. You learn how to apply for it. In effect, you get a tutorial about all the things you need to think about, including the shots that they need, how to get the animal neutered, and why feeding them organic food is better for them.

All this information really helps a person take a step into the journey of owning a pet, rather than just going to a pet shop and feeling worried that they may not understand the whole process.

...AND ROOMS ON THE SPOT

You can even see pop-ups in the home design field! These are often approached from an interior design point of view, but they can also be from a technology point of view. You can have a home where you showcase different kinds of speakers, Wi-Fi capabilities, Bluetooth, television, or touchscreens. Not only can this show customers how the technology is unique, but also how it could integrate seamlessly into their own homes.

When you educate customers, you leave them with an unforgettable impression of your brand — your brand message. They end up with a deeper understanding of who you are and how your products can fit into their lifestyle.

eight

Immersing Your Customer

Whether you have a newly launched company, or an existing business with followers, you will always need to think about what your brand's promise is. Ask yourself, who is my customer? What do they care about? What do they value? Where do they shop now? Where do they eat? Do they care about art? Do they go to museums? Are they avid athletes? Before planning, really think about all of those touch points of the customer.

From there, you should be able to reverse engineer the qualities your space needs to exude. You can say, *"Okay, if this is the kind of person I want to attract, these are the types of things I should be presenting."* It's really got to be about the promise you're delivering and the core values of what your customer cares about. It's just like if you were advertising online. If you think your customer is a big tennis player, or vacations at country clubs, or that he's a big golfer, you want to present the same feel as those things that he already loves. It's all about what you're saying to your customer when they come to this physical space.

Presenting a strong message has always been the province of luxury retailers. A lot of luxury retailers were slower to adopt the pop-up retail strategy and waited longer to invest in these strategies because their high price points don't lend themselves to the impulse buying associated with pop-up shops. Very few people come in off the street and spend $2,000!

However, the lay of the land has changed. Luxury retailers are discovering that pop-ups can accomplish all of these other goals besides short-term revenue, and that cool pop-ups in chic locations can really build a connection by immersing their customers.

CHANEL IN ASPEN, GOOP DELIGHT, HERMES AND HOPSCOTCH

Chanel had a pop-up in Aspen this summer. They determined that customers that shop Chanel are probably vacationing in Aspen, so the location was a good location fit. Their strategy was to create a unique vibe and the luxury lifestyle message: *you're getting to walk into the lifestyle of the Chanel brand.* When you talk about strong messages, that's a great example of one that plays right into many customers' aspirations.

Sometimes, you'll have a pop-up by a luxury brand for their known customers; sometimes, that same brand might use it to be a bit more approachable.

Hermes used this approach and produced a series of pop-up stores in 2014, one of which was at the shops at Columbus Circle, a high-end mall in NYC. They set up a retro diner where you could play hopscotch or a round of mini-golf. For them, it made the brand feel more approachable versus the exclusive image it tends to have. Their message was, *"Okay, we're a luxury brand, and things are always going to have a high-end feeling...but we're also approachable."* They appealed to a larger market by doing pop-ups that were a little bit more fun and interactive and made the brand's message friendlier.

GET THE MESSAGE?

Brand message is the number-one thing that could make or break your company: it's the promise you make to your customer. This has to be really clear. If not, you'll just confuse the customer. To whom are you appealing? Why should they believe in you? Are you marketing a lifestyle, a top-quality product that will last a lifetime, or a product to make my day easier?

For example, West Coast-based Sole Society launched a series of pop-up shops from their Culver City headquarters during the summer months. The first two activations were end of the season sample sales and the final activation was a pre-fall offering. While the value proposition of each pop-up differed in pricing and hook, all stood true to the overall promise of the brand — they believe every woman deserves to look chic and their mission is to surprise and delight with on-trend style from the shoe up (check out the hashtag #mysolesociety and you can see how they consistently convey this message).

CUTTING THROUGH THE ONLINE OVERLOAD

How does this idea differ from what you can offer on your webpage?

Online, customers can visit stores that showcase a specific product line, and then see a list of retailers. But what do you do to draw traffic to your site? You want to have a breadth of product offerings, with fresh content all the time. You want to have a variety of different styles, colors, sizes, and all of that.

Sometimes, though, that's overwhelming. Sometimes, it's just too many choices, and a customer doesn't know how to sift through all of it.

Blame that overload on the way online marketing works now. You have to compete and push content all the time to show up in search engines, and you need to have fresh content for social media every day. Some of it feels like you're addressing customers, but some of it feels like noise.

When you go to an actual physical space, however, you can be super-specific about the conversation that you want to have in that determined timeframe, with specific kinds of customers.

DO MESSAGES ONLY MATTER WITH LUXURY BRANDS?

Not necessarily. There are plenty of non-luxury companies that can create an aspirational message around their brand.

Obviously, Amazon's probably not going to have a pop-up for baking soda (though they do hone in on their strong brand promise to deliver selection, best pricing, and speed of delivery with next-day or same-day shipping and other kinds of distribution benefits), but there are many products that are inexpensive, but unique enough that a pop-up can make sense.

Just because your product isn't Marc Jacobs or Chanel, doesn't mean you can't get your customers excited about your brand.

A brand must always have a message. Whether they are a newly launched start-up company or a luxury brand with an enormous following, having a strong message is central to a brand's influence. It's about getting really specific about what you want to say to your customer and using your pop-up as a way to say it.

DOWN TO CASES: THE TOMMY POP-UP HOUSE, LOUIS VUITTON, AND DOVER STREET

Tommy Hilfiger did a pop-up shop in New York City in the meatpacking district, a very high traffic area of Manhattan, and it was literally a Tommy Hilfiger pop-up house. People were invited to walk into his fabulously preppy summer lifestyle, from boat shoes, to ping pong paddles, to badminton rackets.

You can see a growing number of examples with the luxury brands inviting customers (existing and new) to walk into their lifestyle. Their pop-ups present the customer with a whole world surrounding their products, not just the specific products they offer. These brands both ask and present answers to crucial customer questions:

- What does this person do?
- How do they dress?
- What do they do for hobbies?
- What do they drink?
- What kind of music do they listen to?

And, as part of the Tommy Hilfiger pop-up world, the brand also had some price points that were a little bit more attainable than in their regular stores. They had pieces from as low as $45 ranging to $200 or $300, versus stores with merchandise that's at a less attainable price point to the mass market.

Louis Vuitton has branched into producing pop-up stores as well, and their collaborations have gone well. They partnered with Dover Street, a creative concept store that merges artists and designers in really unique ways. Their goal was to cross into the creative, artistic market, so the Louis Vuitton brand didn't feel like just a high-profile, highbrow luxury brand; it delivered a more artistic approach and interpretation.

While luxury retailers may on average be later to adopt

pop-up shop strategies, they are inherently well-equipped to deliver an elite, high touch experience, and hence, are great examples of immersive retail. They understand they must deliver content that conveys a promise and they must develop a strong customer relationship. The imagery, product quality, and lifestyle message is consistent, and the temporary spaces they create deliver an environment that makes their brand seem more approachable and attainable. Customers are able to step into a world that might have otherwise seemed beyond the realm of possibility. It's this opportunity that opens up possibilities for the development of new brand-consumer relationships.

nine

Forming Partnerships

The Louis Vuitton example discussed in the previous chapter feeds well into the next major purpose of pop-ups: allowing brands to experiment with working with other companies. If brands have overlapping customer bases but don't compete for wallet share, pop-up shops are a great way for them to inexpensively test those partnerships.

Of course, a brand should do their homework ahead of time to make sure that they're aligning themselves with some-body who would appeal to the customer that they want to go after, and that the two brands are delivering similar value propositions even though they make different products. Once that happens, it gives them a way to cross-market each other.

In addition to promoting each other's products, the brand synergy can also amplify the message of the ultimate lifestyle that they're delivering. J.Hilburn did this during their Fortnight in SoHo pop-up, and they had great success bringing in all sorts of strategic partners. For example, one partner was Daniel Wellington watches, which have a very engaged audience on Instagram and other social channels, which paired well with J.Hilburn's extremely strong presence in more traditional media. When J.Hilburn was mentioned in the *Wall Street Journal* and the *New York Times*, or when Daniel Wellington watches were getting attention on their highly engaged social media channels, both parties benefitted. They weren't competing: one sells watches, one sells clothing, but they're appealing to the same type of man.

This situation was further enhanced at the J.Hilburn pop-up by bringing on more partners, all of which targeted the same demographic in order to round out that ideal lifestyle. This included the whiskey that they drank, the bourbon that was served, and the bottled water, which was Fred Water, which is a water bottle shaped like a flask that's branded as very masculine. They had energy-infused turkey jerky. They covered all the bases. What does the brand think you're going to eat, or drink, or do in your life? Having that water bottle, or a sip of that bourbon, or that snack just entrenches in the customer's mind that *this is the life I have if I shop this brand*.

Nike and other athletic companies collaborate a lot as well: Nike × Riccardo Tisci, or Adidas × Stella McCartney, for example. Those collaborations make for great pop-ups because it's introducing a new and unique capsule collection. You're getting the story behind why the design happened or the aesthetic purposes of it or why they combined with that celebrity or designer. Maybe you're getting to meet them as well.

This worked extremely well when Sarah Jessica Parker did her collaboration with Nordstrom. There's a huge, active audience of women who have been watching her on *Sex and the City* for years and coveting her shoes. One day, they were able to go to a pop-up, meet Sarah Jessica Parker, and have her help them try on shoes! Even if they missed it, they were seeing the flurry online of women posting pictures on Instagram of themselves with her, and trying on the shoes. The customer can then check the full collection going forward at Nordstrom.

You often see similar kinds of collaborations happening in other stores as well, such as Target, where it's not a new phenomenon. They've been collaborating with celebrities forever. Target has massive stores where there's a lot going on, and most shoppers could easily miss a new collection. However, Target makes their partnership clear by hosting name-designer-for-Target pop-up stores, where shoppers are able to access a brand that they couldn't normally afford. Target uses these pop-ups to promote their new collaborations, and to test which ones are working best.

CELEBRITY ENDORSEMENTS AND PRODUCTS THAT WALK OUT THE DOOR

When customers get to see a new collaboration firsthand, magic can happen. Brands that partnered with Target knew they would be popular, but when Target partnered with Missoni, they couldn't even get through three days without selling out! That was one of many examples that has taught brands that collaborations with celebrities can happen successfully in an isolated pop-up environment before they actually hit the full stores.

As an added benefit, the brand can see immediately how popular the collaboration is. Depending on how nimble they are (it's probably harder for sneaker brands than clothing brands for example), they can potentially use this information to adjust how they're going to approach merchandising when they actually hit the stores, or potentially do re-orders because they see, in a very isolated test market, how shoppers react.

However, even though pop-ups allow brands to test collaborations more inexpensively, not every celebrity works with every product or every audience. Don't test everything! You still need to be thoughtful.

If you're a brand that price-point wise, aesthetic-wise, and style-wise appeals to a woman whose average age is 40 to 50, and you have Selena Gomez or Miley Cyrus holding your bag, how does that help? You're totally off brand. As a 40-year-old woman, I'm not going to be motivated to dive into that brand because Miley held it.

Now, if your core market was 15 to 20 years old girls, that would be appropriate. Despite being able to test collaborations inexpensively, your first line of defense against bad ideas is your own understanding of your brand. Ideally, your customers should look at all celebrity collaborations and think, *"That's somebody I see as cool. That's somebody I aspire to be like. I value the way they carry themselves in life. If they do this, I'm going to at least try it or look into it, because I align myself with that person."*

So, give careful thought to your collaborations; make them appropriate for your target customer, not just hip with a generic "in crowd" (whatever that is!). Get it wrong and you send a confusing message. Get it right, however, and the products walk out the door. Just ask Target!

PART

III

Pop-Ups A to Z

ten

How Do I Measure ROI?

Regardless of your goals, you will always want to be well positioned to understand the return on investment (ROI) for your pop-up. Obviously, some portion of your ROI is sales, but to see it as only sales is short-sighted. There's a bigger picture that involves building the brand.

If you're thinking, *I really want to do a pop-up, but I'm not really understanding the ROI. Maybe I should just do a trunk show...* then maybe you should. Being in a physical space with your customer is definitely a good way to interact. The part that's missing is the branded element.

When a brand does a pop-up and they think about ROI, often

they literally just think, *how many dollars am I going to make in that space, and is this going to be profitable?* They don't think, *how many dollars are going to come in the door over the six months because of my two-week or one-month pop-up?*

Because it's a short-term experience that should have a long-term impact, you can't just examine immediate sales when you consider a pop-up's ROI. You need to think about:

» *Is the pop-up increasing sales?*
» *Is the pop-up increasing marketing awareness?*
» *Is the pop-up allowing us to better demonstrate our product?*

You need to remember there's a difference between qualitative benefits and sales. Qualitative benefits can eventually *lead to more sales*, but they're not the same thing.

For example, you can use your POS system and sensory technology to learn, as discussed in Chapter 6. Or you can utilize this pop-up experience to increase brand awareness by putting proper incentives in place to get people to speak about your brand over social channels as discussed in Chapter 5.

There's ROI in all of that because if, over a four-day period, you get 100 people to talk about your brand who hadn't before, then you have 100 people times all their followers who have now learned about your brand. That's worth something. That is a return on your investment. Not only are they sharing it, but afterward, you can follow up and see who those people were, who they engaged with, and to whom you can further reach out.

In order to really capitalize on that benefit, you need to be sure to have to have systems in place to track this information. Most of these systems are relatively basic, like getting Google Analytics set up and understanding where your drivers of traffic are coming from, or going back to your own social channels and seeing what new engagement happened and how many times you were mentioned over the time period of your pop-up.

You can also see what people are gravitating to, what was catching their attention. That can give you merchandising feedback, which is also hugely important. What you're going to order for next season, what styles are the most popular, what you're going to put on your homepage, what's going to be part of your email marketing — all that is a return on your investment.

On the demonstration or customer feedback side, you're demoing a product in a retail setting and getting to see what people like, what they do and don't understand, where they have questions, and what is influencing them to convert or not to convert to a sale. Although it's difficult to calculate, you can be sure that all provides an ROI for a brand from merchandising, manufacturing, and marketing points of view.

On the educational side, the pop-up helps a customer have a deeper relationship with the brand, because they're learning so much more about the company and the products. It can add to that "wow" factor and make someone more likely to share your brand's content.

On a manufacturing side, you can realize a customer might really love your product and certain aspects of it. You might have put the bells and whistles on it because you thought those were going to make them really excited, but you learn that they're not willing to pay more for them. If they would buy the product regardless, at a certain price point that's lower, you'll learn not to manufacture the rest of the line with those bells and whistles. That can save you money, and that contributes to ROI.

Pop-ups can also teach you about your customers by studying the flow of traffic. What leads customers from one area of purchase to the next? When most people buy X product, is their next step is to look at Y product based on that information? You can use this information not only to create your in-store experience, but also to design your web presence.

In a sense, these are all qualitative benefits, but longer-term. If done well, they should have a quantitative benefit over the next season or two.

BIG CROWD = BIG ROI?

Drawing a lot of people is great, but brands also need to keep in mind that they need to be very specific in their goals, and they need to deliver something that feels thought-out, purposeful, and authentic. People love to walk into a space that feels worth remembering. The customers always need a hook. Now, that hook doesn't always have to be a sale or a deal, but there's got to be something that you create that resonates with them and lures them into wanting to buy-in to your brand.

That memorable experience touches on everything: the design, the flow, the curation of the merchandise in the space. In today's day and age, people love having a voice, so can you empower them to participate in a conversation about your brand? How, in this time period, will you create what feels like a VIP relationship with your customer? Customers are more likely to come back and to follow you online because, in your pop-up space, they felt something that was a little bit more VIP, a little bit more special, a little bit more unique than they would have gotten by just stepping into any store that day or that week.

By realizing that your pop-up has goals besides drawing the biggest crowd possible, you can optimize for those goals.

When a company's trying to figure out the key performance indicators (KPIs) for their pop-up, it's important to realize how valuable all of these qualitative benefits are. There are a lot of different things they can think about, including social media, data, product, sentiment, and all of the other factors discussed above.

A pop-up is not just about sales. All of the qualitative indicators and leading indicators mentioned in this chapter will lead to benefits down the road. Although it's difficult to calculate, ultimately, these pieces are added together to answer the question, "What's the ROI?"

eleven

The How-to Guide:
Q & A for Your Pop-Up Experience

This book is not meant to be a how-to guide. Others have tackled this concept. The purpose of this chapter is to provide you as the reader with a brief overview of the things you should be thinking about as you move forward, and some basic best practices for each step.

SHOULD I PUT ON A POP-UP?
If you came to me and asked, "Should I put on a pop-up?" I would answer, "That depends." There are so many factors affecting whether or not a pop-up is a good idea that there is no one-size-fits-all answer. The easiest way to tackle the situation is to come at it backwards.

Here are some reasons why your brand might not be ready for a pop-up:

- If you have zero idea of what your retail strategy is, don't do a pop-up. The companies that have effective pop-ups are the ones that understand their overall retail strategy. They know why they're doing a pop-up. They have a clear message. Sometimes, that's trickier than it sounds: a brand can have a really cool idea, but it's still confused.
- If you don't know what customer you're going after, don't do a pop-up. Even if your suppositions turn out wrong, you can learn through a pop-up that your customer is somebody different. However, if you don't have a clear initial point of view, don't do it.
- If you don't understand what you're asking a customer to do and what you're giving back for it, don't do a pop-up. You're selling an experience to a customer, not just a product. If you don't understand what that experience is, your call to action, and what you're giving back, a pop-up will waste your time and money.
- If your idea is so complicated that you can't explain it to me in a sentence, don't do a pop-up. Something that complicated or muddled will be lost on the customer. He or she won't understand it.

If you do understand your general retail strategy, customer, and product, the next step is to think about your goals.

Ask yourself: why do you want to do a pop-up? What do you want to get out of it? Sales is always a piece of the puzzle, but it is rarely the biggest motivator. Is it brand awareness? Do you need to grow your social media following? Do you need to educate your customers? Do you want to experiment?

If your answer to the question, "Why do I want to do a pop-up?" is one of the topics discussed so far in this book, it's likely that a pop-up is a good choice.

SO WHERE DO I START?

Start figuring out your pop-up strategy by answering a few basic questions:

1. **What are you looking to achieve?** What are your goals? This should be the same answer you came up with in the last section.
2. **Why do you want to do a pop-up, specifically?** Is there another way to achieve the same goals? Is doing a pop-up your most effective option?
3. **What's the end goal?** What exactly would success look like? What are the specific things you'd like your pop-up to accomplish?

Using these answers, you should have a pretty clear idea of what your pop-up is trying to achieve. This is when strategizing becomes more of an art than a science. You'll need to be creative in coming up with the most unique and effective way to achieve those goals. This could be something as straightforward as a standard, well-branded pop-up, or as crazy as some of the more unique pop-ups discussed in this book. The only rule is that it should achieve your goals.

WHAT'S THE AVERAGE COST OF SETTING UP A POP-UP STORE?

This is a tricky question to answer, as there are so many variables that impact budgeting. While we can't give an average without at least assessing the brand, industry category, goals, and inventory, there are buckets where your money will go. Use these buckets as a way to roughly calculate costs.

What are the basic buckets involved in a pop-up budget?

⇢ **Rent**
⇢ **WiFi**
⇢ **Alarm System and Security**
⇢ **Insurance**
⇢ **Inventory Packaging**
⇢ **Merchandising Fixtures**
⇢ **Paint and Decor**
⇢ **Staffing**
⇢ **Marketing**
⇢ **Opening Reception**
⇢ **Finding Sponsors**
⇢ **Gifts for Influencers**

If you don't have enough for all those buckets, you're going to sell yourself short. Be careful: it can be useless, or even harmful, to have a pop-up that's unimpressive.

By the time you factor in the time, the space, the rent, et

al., if you don't have a minimum budget around $15,000–$20,000 — and that's a low budget — then you're probably better off doing a trunk show to start.

On the other end of the spectrum, with $150,000 to $300,000, you can have more of a branded impact. Of course, there are even larger budgets to, say, redesign a shipping container, travel city-to-city, and really create something innovative, but a six figure budget is more than enough to do something really effective and creative.

LOCATION, LOCATION, LOCATION

Location is one of the biggest decisions a prospective pop-up will make. Depending on factors like where your customer is shopping now and what their average price point is, you can start to figure out which areas might be most appealing to them.

The first step is to decide on a neighborhood. Where in the city your pop-up is located will make all the difference in who shows up. A lot of traffic that your pop-up will bring in is foot traffic, and even engaged customers often won't be willing to travel across the city to get to your location. Think carefully about which area makes the most sense for your demographic.

Once you've decided on a neighborhood, deciding on a space is mostly a matter of budget.

BUDGET RULES!

The amount of merchandise you want to include and what you want to do in the space will determine how much space you need. However, budget determines all of this because you may be priced out of some locations.

However, as always, keep your customer in mind. Do they care about a polished, gallery feel, or would they be okay with more of an unfinished, rustic feel? Affordable larger spaces are often available if you're able to do something funky with them that might appeal to your customer.

THE NITTY-GRITTY OF CHOOSING A SPACE

Once you understand all of this, it's time to start hunting for spaces. Here are the practical things to think about when looking at a space:

What does your rent include? Does it include electricity, water, or other services? Is there a utility fee? Do you need a security deposit? Will you have Wi-Fi available? Are there alarm systems? How about bathrooms? Will you need to build dressing rooms? Does the site have a liquor license? Do you have to get one? Are there any permits required?

You should take some time studying the foot traffic of the area to determine busy times of the day, and if there will be any restrictions on store hours based on the landlord or the neighbors. Also, make sure you talk to the landlord ahead of time about whether you can paint the walls, or hang things, and what the rules are pertaining to signage in the windows.

You really want to work with a space that's at street level, that allows you to have signage, and that doesn't have scaffolding. All those things can make a big difference. You can probably find a cheaper space that's on the second floor or has scaffolding, but you're really working against yourself. Unless you have such a huge following already that no matter where you go, you're going to be able to drive traffic, take your street presence seriously. Because a pop-up exists for an isolated small period of time, it can be easily thwarted with the wrong space.

THE REST OF THE NITTY-GRITTY

Every detail in a pop-up matters. Once you have the space, the real planning begins.

The first things to think about are the design, the paint, the decorative elements, and the merchandising fixtures that will personalize it. You want to think about your inventory packaging, as well as the bags or boxes that your customers are going to walk out with.

You'll also need to think of staffing. Remember, you don't just want salespeople; you want ambassadors of the brand. Marketers and merchandisers alike should all be able to tell the brand story, really understand why this activation is happening, understand how to collect data from the customers entering the space, and how to better service or share that data with the company or the brand.

Furthermore, don't underestimate exterior and interior signage — ever. There should be clear signage. Use the word pop-up. Let people know it's short-term. Be clear on the dates, times, and where customers can find you online.

Another underrated element is to decorate the window nicely. Tell a lifestyle story that's very specific. Don't simply say it's Christmas. Maybe tie in *The Nutcracker*. Don't just say it's summer. Have a very specific beach scene. The window is really important.

Make sure that as soon as customers walk in the door, they get an immersive experience that's very clear about what your brand stands for. Something that resonates with them, evokes some sort of emotion, and dives deep into the authenticity of the brand. Is your customer a huge soccer fan? Do they love to play golf or polo? Think about all of the lifestyle elements that you can tie in with your message.

In order to accomplish this, think about collaborations that are compatible with the goal you have for the pop-up in the first place. You could do a pop-up as a single brand where you're the main focus and bring in strategic partners, or you can do a collaborative pop-up. Maybe you don't feel like you have enough inventory to fill a full space, or you want to collaborate with other brands to amplify your marketing reach. It's also nice to share the costs, pool efforts on acquiring fixtures, merchandising, and designing the space. However, beware that this really only works if the brands have similar goals, align themselves to create a cohesive branded experience, and attract the same customer but don't compete with you for wallet share.

Instead of having a pop-up shop of all ties, for example, you could have one brand with shoes, one brand with ties, and one brand with button-down shirts. You might bring in a coffee vendor so that it's more of a holistic experience for your target customer. Then co-marketing really works to your benefit, because you're cross-marketing the same kind of consumer, but you probably have different followings at the time of the opening because you have different products.

Whether you're a solo act or part of a collaboration, make sure that you have a number of eye-catching displays sprinkled throughout the store so that you're keeping customers engaged and moving. Make sure there are a myriad of opportunities to re-engage with the customer and catch his or her attention, through either traditional fixtures and displays or innovative ideas like augmented reality and technology.

All this will remind your customers multiple times what they should do, making sure that your calls to action are clear. The call to action will be sales at some point, but if it's marketing-oriented and you want them to participate in a conversation, make sure that that's really clearly stated throughout the store as well.

Also, ensuring that you have a POS system set up is important. This depends on both your budget and what other info you'd like to collect on the spot, so you can create and select other data. For example, companies like Footmarks, Indoo.rs, and Swarm Mobile allow you to tie foot traffic to the time of day and conversion rates of sales. Consider employing some of those options to learn more about your customers shopping patterns.

And remember that even though it's temporary, the most

successful pop-ups we work on are those where people can't believe it's temporary because it looks so finished and so professional. It's something they can believe in and invest in as a brand, because it has such a finished feel, even though it's only going to be there for a short period of time.

ZERO HOUR: MANAGING THE POP-UP OPENING DAY
When the critical opening day approaches, people always freak out. That's not unusual. Even though it's planned, a pop-up is also in some senses a live event. There are always going to be things that come up. We always recommend people give themselves a little wiggle room for build-out.

Let's say you're planning on a month-long pop-up with a build-out on Monday. Don't plan your opening reception until Wednesday night; that way you have two full days in the space. You can do a soft opening if you're ready on Tuesday, but you're probably going to want to move things around a number of times, and you don't want to be hurried.

Also, don't forget to account for Murphy's Law. Things happen. You might be having an opening reception and a huge storm comes up, and you can't control it. The power could go out, or some other damage might happen. Be open-minded and have a backup plan of another day that you can plan an event. If Wi-Fi is not working, have a backup plan for how you're going to run sales.

There are always glitches that happen, so give yourself a cushion in the front end. Building out the store is almost always going to take two to three times as long as your break-down day.

Also, unless you're going to a street fair or you're a huge brand that everybody already knows, over time your traction will increase. Don't expect to open doors and all of a sudden be sold out of product. It happens, but it's rare. Think of it as planting seeds every single day that you're there with people in the neighborhood, letting them know that doors are open so word continues to spread and people continue to come back.

The nice thing about a pop-up is that people seem to be more flexible with them, more understanding. Brands have had to open up a little later than expected because build-up didn't go as smoothly, or maybe their product is coming in from overseas and they were caught in customs and they don't have their full offering but the store doors are open. That can be devastating for a brand, but you can still walk them through your website. You can still tell them the story. You can still let them know about the other products you have.

Maybe you need to get them to come back in and you let them know, "I'm sorry this hasn't arrived yet, but if you come back, I'll give you 15 percent off." No matter what goes wrong, as long as a brand is always thinking about how they can make it better for the customer so that they feel like they're being treated like a VIP and loyalist for being patient, it will go a long way. For the most part, everything works itself out over the duration of the pop-up.

READY TO GET STARTED?

If you're eager to delve further into the nitty-gritty of your pop-up, there's a book you can use to learn more. It's called *Pop-Up Business for Dummies*. If you want to handle running a pop-up on your own, then that book is the best place to turn to learn how.

If you are too busy to handle all the details of your pop-up and want someone with experience to handle and optimize the entire process for you, there are plenty of experts who can help, including my firm, The Lion'esque Group.

One thing that's certain, we're seeing people do pop-ups now across the board for all sorts of reasons. We have helped a client produce a cupcake pop-up, Google did a pop-up in San Francisco, restaurants collaborate with magazines to do six-month pop-ups and bring in celebrity chefs. The design firm Gensler even did a pop-up law firm in D.C. Pop-Up law. Yes, indeed — it's all about knowing what you want to accomplish with this limited-time, limited-scope experience.

Determine your reasons, be clear-eyed about what you want to accomplish, and you're already halfway to a successful pop-up hit.

twelve

Creating Buzz

You have the message down, the space and design is determined, and now it's time to plan your calendar of events and marketing strategy. Before getting started on marketing your pop-up shop, it's important to remember that regardless of the campaign you're launching, the messages you send need to have a strong hook, create urgency and target people that write about the product or promise you're selling.

Remember, today people are communicating publicly all the time about their feelings, what they value, and what they're looking for. If you can proactively find a few communicators that meet your target demographic, then you can target them as brand evangelists for your pop-up activation. These are the really hardcore communicators. They're on the front line and they're engaged with their following. You can start letting them know ahead of time by saying, "Hey, this is opening, and we'd like to send you a special invitation."

BEFORE LAUNCH, FOCUS ON YOUR SPECIFIC CAMPAIGN

First off, let's dispel all rumors: traditional media is not dead. Just like people still love shopping at retail and pop-up shops, they will continue to watch TV and read print magazines, and they still enjoy attending in-person meet-ups and conferences.

Now, when it comes to targeting traditional media, the key point to keep in mind is knowing what your customer reads, and targeting editors that cover the right beat. Sounds basic, right? But to effectively target traditional media outlets, be sure to remember two basic principles: 1) make their job easier by pitching content they can use; and 2) know their publishing timelines.

You can accomplish this by thinking through the angle that a journalist could use to write about your pop-up that would appeal to their readers. Don't think about why you want them to write about you. Instead, think about why readers would want to read about your pop-up. If you can explain this to them, journalists will be thrilled to promote your story.

Next, it's important to get influencers to become your evangelists. How do you get them to visit your shop, snap a photo, post it on their Instagram, and hopefully blog about your store?

The easiest way to explain is with an example: Say you were doing a pop-up with one of the major sportswear or sports gear companies during the World Cup. You can pro-actively search for conversations based on key words your potential customer cares about, as they are talking about the #WorldCup. They could be talking about a specific team that's competing in the World Cup, or about a specific athlete who plays on that team. Get into the conversation, and you'll get into their world.

Think of influencers as press. They want to know *what's hot, what's new, what's fresh* first, just as a reporter would, and if you can deliver that message to him or her, you can capture your next fan. Have a list of your key targets and be realistic.

1. Find influencers who write about your price point (i.e., a blogger that writes about TJMaxx finds and Target scores is probably not going to cover a new handbag launch where the price point is $700+ because it's not what their readers value, nor can afford).
2. Have a budget for gifting. Win him or her over with samples that they can touch, feel, and wear publicly.
3. Present them with the opportunity to offer an exclusive discount code to their readers if they shop at your pop-up store. (Be sure each individual is given a unique code.)
4. Invite them to co-host a night at your pop-up shop on a night of their choice and make the event center around them and their sense of style.

A lot of the time, you'll invite influencers and press before your doors officially open. They'll come in the night before it opens to the public and then tell all of their followers why they must visit this new shop.

Once the seeds are planted with editors and influencers, it's time to start watering your seeds with a social media strategy. Social media can feel daunting for a first time pop-up, but just like you make an editorial calendar for press deadlines, make an editorial calendar for your social strategy across relevant channels.

1. Start with a key word document, a database you can refer back to with words that align with your pop-up goals, brand message, values, and promise.
2. Create one hashtag to help you track your campaign leading up to, during, and after your pop-up store is open.
3. Make an editorial calendar that includes a countdown and new announcements throughout your pop-up campaign, and have someone on your team who is prepared to track and engage with followers.

If you have strategic partners, such as a watch brand or a food brand, you should pre-craft the language you're all going to share across social channels, not just your own. One example is a partnership like Missoni for Target; the merchandise doesn't hit Target stores until a week later, but because of this two- or three-day pop-up shop that sold out, by the time it gets to Target, people will be lining up out the door. People can't wait to get it because in the first three-day opportunity, it sold out and both partners were talking about it across their channels. Now there's anxiety: *"I need to have this product."*

KEY BUZZWORD: "FOR A LIMITED TIME ONLY"
A pop-up engenders a feeling of urgency. Customers feel that they are limited by time and inventory, so they are motivated

to take action. As long as the brand has a clear message, because of the timeframe that they're there, this urgency only enhances the experience and stresses to the customers that they need to *get it now* or they won't have an opportunity to get it again, at least, not *in the same kind of way*. That's key.

DON'T BE THE LAST ONE ON YOUR BLOCK!

Apple is a perfect example of a brand that plays into this phenomenon all the time. People feel like they must have the next Mac or iPhone iteration first. Apple will host a media event where they give little info and show teasers of the upgrade to come — and everyone from Tech Crunch to Engadget writes about it — and then everybody wants it.

So how does your brand create the "Apple buzz"?

You play into knowing that people inherently hate missing out on things (hence the popular hashtag #**fomo**). You can always see your friends tomorrow, but it's hard to resist seeing them at this great party tonight with all the other cool people going. You don't want to miss out on a good deal, either, especially if it's for a very limited time.

That's how it worked with the Daisy Marc Jacobs pop-up store. No matter how many times they went to the Marc Jacobs store a few blocks away the following week, they wouldn't have the same experience that they got in those three days where they could participate in the conversation and get free products for it. They could hear DJ Jilly Hendrix spinning, have coffee from a solar-powered coffee truck, get free manicures and see great artwork by Langley Fox Hemingway. They had an opportunity to engage with the brand in a way that they wouldn't be able to do the next week.

Technology has also really caught up to the *here now, gone tomorrow* retail world, allowing brands to be more creative and make something unique in physical spaces. It's really bridging the two worlds. Social media has empowered the industry in a way that couldn't happen five or ten years ago. Brands can post where they can be found, and customers create tons of user-generated content into their own channels. Whether it's in a truck, or in a traditional brick-and-mortar space, social media has really enabled people to drive traffic to wherever they are now.

GETTING YOUR GOOD NEWS ON THE STREET

There are dozens of influencers that could be champions for the brand leading up to and during the pop-up. The best combinations pair up social media and online chatter with good old-fashioned guerrilla marketing. Create postcards with a clear call to action and coupon code for visiting and place them at nearby outlets with a similar clientele to your target market.

Here are some ideas:

- Are there hotels nearby with concierge desks?
- Are there any service-oriented stores nearby that cater to your customers?
- Are there any other businesses nearby that your audience frequents?

- How else can you let people in the neighborhood know that you're there?

These old-school traditional tactics still really work!

PROMOTIONAL EFFORTS FROM THE OUTSIDE IN

The marketing of your product and brand message doesn't stop when someone enters your pop-up. In fact, that's when it truly begins. Whether it's you or hired brand ambassadors staffing the store, you will want to be sure that the right thought process and training is invested for the faces of your storefront.

Choose employees who represent the aesthetic of your brand to run your pop-up store, and make a point of investing time to ensure they understand the brand promise, can explain the unique value proposition of what you sell, and are a further extension of you.

The Pop-Up Marketing Checklist:

- **Get Going with Influencers.** Start by creating a list of the key target influencers and bloggers you want to see at you pop-up and reach out to them by highlighting different incentives for them to get involved.
- **Build Anticipation with Social Media.** Social media can feel daunting for a first-time pop-up, but just as you'd make an editorial calendar for press deadlines, make an editorial calendar for your social strategy with all the social platforms on which you plan to be active.
- **Use Traditional Media.** Traditional media is still a great way to get attention and let people know that your pop-up is happening. Just remember to start early.
- **Activate Partners.** Bringing the right partners on board will give you access to an entirely new audience of their fans.
- **Take to the Streets.** Create postcards with a clear call to action and coupon code for visiting your pop-up and place them at nearby outlets with a similar clientele to your target market.
- **Hire the Right Staff.** Giving customers an amazing experience is what leads to the best marketing of all: word of mouth.

PART

IV

What's Still to Come?

thirteen

The Face of the Retail Future

The only thing certain about retail's evolution now is that it's not going anywhere, aided and abetted by technology that allows it to become totally immersive in ways you might find hard to believe — until you're in the middle of them! Whether it's in a temporary store or permanent one, the emergence of online, mobile and physical commerce continues to evolve. Here are a few areas currently developing that we find exciting.

BEHIND THE BRAND EXPERIENCES WITH AUGMENTED REALITY

Augmented Reality is where some elements actually exist in a physical space, while others are accessed via your phone.

With a few taps, customers can get deeper information on a product. Customers can see additional in-depth information or a wider array of products, all with the touch of a couple of keys. There doesn't even have to be a salesperson with them; they can get the story of a brand, how a product was created, analysis of materials or processes, you name it. It's a futuristic approach to shopping, where the consumer is more educated and savvy than at any time in retail history.

Today we are seeing early examples of this with companies like Bauble Bar working with Perch Interactive to extend their merchandise offerings or companies like Airwalk working with Snaps, which created a virtual pop-up store within a geo-fenced area in Washington Square Park in New York City.

It doesn't stop there. There are also apps that allow you to see how a garment will potentially look on you without even putting it on through an app that simulates the image. Warby Parker are masters at this with their virtual Try-On technology to select the ideal glasses for your face shape. Makeup companies, such as Maybelline with their FitMe™ app, use this to help women find the perfect foundation for their skin tone. Uniqlo has worked this into their stores with their Magic Mirror that helps shoppers decide which item to buy by using a touchscreen that prompts you to select additional hue offerings of a jacket you are trying on and projects your modified reflection back to you.

This isn't the future — it's already here!

WHITE-GLOVE SERVICE: BEACON TECHNOLOGY

While augmented reality is dynamic, brands can also connect what we call beacon technology.

The best way to explain beacon technology is to picture yourself embarking on your honeymoon. You arrive at the Four Seasons Hotel front door and the doorman greets you by name. The concierge already has your favorite drinks ready to go, handing them to you as you're checking in. Everything is perfect and exactly to your taste — a high-touch "white glove" kind of service that you'd think people would have to be telepathic to accomplish. But they don't: all they need to do is have you set up in the store's beacon system and you can be treated to the same kind of experience when you step into your favorite retailer.

You already can see samples of this online. When you shop, you get messages that say something along the lines of, "Based on what you're looking at, we recommend these other products." This beacon technology even goes a step further than that, however, by combining GPS coordinates to literally send you welcoming messages when you step into the store and alert you to special sales, or the ingredients list for a specific product. The possibilities are almost endless, and they're being integrated into brick-and-mortar stores now as a "preferred customer" benefit that is a holistic, pampering experience.

Of course, beacon technology is definitely in its infancy. People are still getting their heads around the idea of indoor mapping technology. But it isn't new. You can go and look at Google Maps on your phone and watch yourself walk through a mall. This new approach simply integrates that with delivering messages to customers, and that's how that's going to evolve.

Eventually, beacon technology could evolve to the point that it's like the Tom Cruise movie *Minority Report*, in which mannequins actually speak to you with customized messages. Some mannequins already have sensors that can see who's in front of them, so don't expect custom conversation to be so far behind.

WINDOWS THAT DELIVER: SHOPPABLE WALLS

Another evolving development on the retail front is shoppable windows and walls. Kate Spade did this in a pop-up in New York City, where customers could walk by the store and see from the outside window all the products being offered. Through a touchscreen, you could shop on the spot and have a messenger deliver the merchandise to you within a couple of hours!

A bookstore in Canada offered a similar experience with a shoppable wall. College students could come, booklists in hand, and click their choices on an interactive wall. Books were bought and delivered shortly thereafter.

In reality, of course, you're not always going to shop this way. Many of us are still fans of brick-and-mortar stores, of overflowing counters just full of treasures to touch and bargains to hunt. But for a busy student, a mother of small children, or a person for whom shopping is challenging, online shopping is extremely convenient — and pop-ups or other outlets with these shoppable interactive features are customizable to you, bridging the gap between the physical brick-and-mortar and your online shopping experience.

Technology continues to develop new experiences that benefit the customer, because that's really what it's there for. Shopping gets more and more personalized as retailers get better in communicating with and delivering to their customers, whether it's a contest, product information, coupons, loyalty codes, or advertisements.

PRINT ON DEMAND

Imagine inventory management solved because you could live create product upon demand in-store. Thanks to companies like MakerBot, in just a few short years since inception, everything from clothing and cars to musical instruments and even body parts can be created with a 3D printer today. Printing in 3D is a common tool for prototyping, but it only recently gained traction among manufacturers and retailers. It enables companies to create and deliver products in small quantities in real time, providing actionable insight into which products will actually drive demand.

In July of 2014, Amazon announced the first Amazon 3D Printing Store where customers could shop among 200 unique products that could be 3D printed on demand and shipped immediately. Customers could choose a ready-made design, or customize it by changing the material, size, style, or color, and then add personalized text or images. Currently, customers shop for jewelry, home decor, toys, and tech accessories.

Think of 3D printing as a factory in the cloud that allows a retailer to offer hundreds or thousands of additional stock keeping units (SKUs) to its customers without requiring more space for inventory. Seems too good to be true? According to a report from ReportBuyer, the worldwide demand for 3D printing is projected to rise more than 20 percent per year — to $5 billion in 2017.

A BRAVE NEW WORLD

Technology continues to evolve and some creations being tried out are so new that they can freak us out. Brands and retailers are going to continue to learn how to understand what's happening in their physical space, whether that's by sensing heat, talking to people's phones, watching for buying patterns, or any number of other metrics. It's really enhancing the digital intelligence in a physical space.

It can feel a little crazy, and it will turn people off unless retailers do a good job of thinking of the customer first and really utilizing it in a way that the customer understands its purpose and intent and appreciates its value. If it serves a customer well, it'll overcome the creepiness. If brands do it right, emphasizing that it's a way to understand the customer and the things they appreciate, it'll foster loyalty to such a degree that brands may not be able to imagine it just yet.

The exciting thing about all this is…it's still evolving. Next year, when we have this same conversation, we'll be talking about even better shopping experiences, even more interaction, and even better ways to delight customers.

Conclusion

Day in and day out, founders, marketers, and investors alike call The Lion'esque Group office inquiring about a pop-up. *How much do they cost? How do we get started?* Somehow the phrase "pop-up shop" has developed a certain level of cache and it's ingrained in every potential retailer's mind.

Well, it can be. However, like all initiatives that are successful, it takes planning to achieve optimal execution. You have to think through the goals, your customer demographic, the brand voice, and, of course, budget. A pop-up shop may be short in duration, but the planning is not and the opportunity cost of the time it takes can be high if you don't properly plan.

Despite the challenge, pop-up shops aren't going anywhere. They aren't a fad that will pass with time or a trend that will be replaced. They are a fundamental answer to the problem of retail in the age of the internet: *How can brands use their in-person time to create the deepest possible relationship with their customers?*

As e-commerce continues to become the norm, shoppers are craving a human connection with the brands they interact with. Sure, some brands can afford year-round physical locations to interact with their customers. But there is also a different experience that is created with a limited time, isolated store experience. For brands with existing storefronts, like Marc Jacobs, it allows them to hone in on a specific target audience with a key message and immersive experience. For other brands, that can not yet afford long term leases, pop-up shops are one of the most affordable, effective answers for brands looking to build a deep emotional connection with their customers.

Pop-ups are not just short-term replacements for retail locations. They can serve not only as a way for brands to create sales, but also to increase customer engagement, learn about their customers, teach their customers about their product, and test partnerships with other brands.

As discussed in this book, pop-up shops are about creating an experience that allows you to connect with customers in a physical space that communicates your brand messaging. They are about telling a story customers will buy into and remember. Despite the limited time frame, pop-up visitors are so absorbed in the lifestyle that the brand represents that the message sticks, often more deeply than it would from the slow, constant exposure of traditional retail.

This is why pop-up shops are one of the fastest growing segments in retail. Customers in an online world crave experiential retail, and pop-ups are the way for brands to focus on telling a story that their customers can truly buy into and remember.

And we're just getting started.

resources and links

CHAPTER 1

http://mashable.com/2013/03/12/forrester-u-s-ecommerce-forecast-2017

http://www.businessinsider.com/shopping-malls-are-going-extinct-2014-1

http://fortunedotcom.files.wordpress.com/2014/05/srr.mediakit2013.pdf

CHAPTER 3

http://www.pinterest.com/nordstrom

CHAPTER 5

#CliquotMail

http://blog.forbestravelguide.com/veuve-clicquot-pop-up-bar-returns-to-aspen-mountain

http://bizbash.com/veuve-clicquots-pop-lounge-champagne-bar-mobile-food-truck-lounge/gallery/82765

http://www.usatoday.com/story/life/movies/2014/07/17/jon-favreau-chef-el-jefe-roy-choi/12729217

http://www.wwd.com/people-companies?lc=int_mb_1001

http://shop.nordstrom.com/c/pop-in-olivia-kim

http://lionesque.tumblr.com/post/83839330019/success-from-failures

CHAPTER 6

http://en.wikipedia.org/wiki/Social_media

http://en.wikipedia.org/wiki/Twitter

http://lionesque.tumblr.com/post/83839330019/success-from-failures

CHAPTER 7

http://www.instyle.com/instyle/look-of-the-day/designer/0,,jennifer-meyer_30197532,00.html

http://www.instyle.com/instyle/look-of-the-day/designer/0,,michael-kors_30205859,00.html

http://www.instyle.com/instyle/look-of-the-day/designer/0,,stella-mccartney_30205857,00

http://www.instyle.com/instyle/look-of-the-day/designer/0,,cushnie-et-ochs_30179074,00.html

CHAPTER 9

http://www.shopify.com/blog/12847177-how-to-land-your-business-in-the-press-6-tactics-and-5-tools

CHAPTER 13

https://www.reportbuyer.com/business_government/printing/world_3d_printing_market.html

Made in the USA
Charleston, SC
04 December 2014